Click

LIGHT
IS ALL AROUND US

BY WENDY PFEFFER · ILLUSTRATED BY PAUL MEISEL

HARPER

An Imprint of HarperCollinsPublishers

Special thanks to Russell P. Leslie, ALA, FIES, Professor and Associate Director, Lighting Research Center, Rensselaer Polytechnic Institute, for his valuable assistance.

The Let's-Read-and-Find-Out Science book series was originated by Dr. Franklyn M. Branley, Astronomer Emeritus and former Chairman of the American Museum of Natural History–Hayden Planetarium, and was formerly co-edited by him and Dr. Roma Gans, Professor Emeritus of Childhood Education, Teachers College, Columbia University. Text and illustrations for each of the books in the series are checked for accuracy by an expert in the relevant field. For more information about Let's-Read-and-Find-Out Science books, write to HarperCollins Children's Books, 195 Broadway, New York, NY 10007, or visit our website at www.letsreadandfindout.com.

Let's Read-and-Find-Out Science® is a trademark of HarperCollins Publishers.

Light Is All Around Us

Library of Congress Cataloging-in-Publication Data is available.

ISBN 978-0-06-238189-7 (trade bdg.) — ISBN 978-0-06-238190-3 (pbk.)

The artist used pen and ink, watercolor, liquid acrylic, pencils, and pastels on Arches watercolor paper to create the illustrations for this book.

15 16 17 18 19   SCP   10 9 8 7 6 5 4 3 2 1
❖
Revised edition, 2015

For my friend, Andrzej
—W.P.

For my light, my family
—P.M.

8

Light is found in many different forms and many different places. It travels from the sun and the stars. It lights up the sky, the sea, and our backyards.

Windows glow. Car lights shine. Signs flash on and off. Bridge lights sparkle. Sometimes, jagged bolts of lightning fill the sky and brightly colored fireworks explode on the Fourth of July.

During the day, light from the sun brightens our world. But the sun is 93 million miles away. How does its light get here?

Light travels to Earth in waves of electromagnetic radiation, a kind of energy that travels through space. These waves travel so fast, we can't even see them move.

light from Earth could travel back

8 miles a minute

1 mile a minute

Cars on highways travel about one mile a minute.

Passenger jet planes travel 8 miles a minute.

14

MINUTE

and forth to the moon 46 times.

13 miles
a minute

RRRRRRRR

11 million miles
a minute

Sound waves travel 13 miles a minute. Light travels over
11 *million* miles a minute. Nothing travels faster than light.

In addition to measuring how fast light is, we can also measure it to find out how bright it is.

To find out how long something is, we measure it in inches.

To find out how hot something is, we measure it in degrees. We measure time in minutes and weight in pounds.

17

Light is measured in lumens. A lightbulb used for reading is usually 1,750 lumens. Sunlight is 35,000,000,000,000,000,000,000,000,000 lumens.

That's 35 octillion lumens, more than all the lightbulbs on
Earth turned on at the same time. That's why you should never
look directly at the sun. It can hurt your eyes.

The sun sends the brightest light, but not all light comes from the sun.

People build fires, light candles, or turn on electric lights.

Some people use a night-light
in their bedroom.

Sometimes, flashlights light the way in the dark.

People in the West Indies used to poke holes in gourds, fill them with fireflies, and use them as flashlights at night.

Just as fireflies glow in the dark, some fish glow in the water. They light up to find a mate, confuse enemies, or lure food.

An octopus has been discovered that glows.
Its blue-green light attracts tiny sea animals.

The octopus's blue-green glow is a chemical light, like the yellow-green glow sticks children carry on Halloween.

Light is important. It lets us see.

Close your eyes.

Since all the light can't get into your eyes,
you don't see all that's around you.

Open your eyes.
Light comes into your eyes and you
see the world with its beautiful colors.

Here's how light helps you see. When light waves hit an object, they bounce off. When they bounce off, we say they "reflect." "Reflect" means that they change direction.

You see a cat because light waves reflect off the cat to your eyes.

Your EYE

Muscle

Lens

Pupil

Retina

Optic Nerve

Cornea

Iris

Light waves enter your eye through the pupil in the center of the colored iris. The waves pass through the lens and form a picture on the retina at the back of your eye. Nerves carry the picture to your brain. And it tells you what you see.

Day or night, light helps us watch the world and its wonders.

Just look and see.

DANGER ALLIGATORS

Find Out More About Light

GREEN PLANTS NEED LIGHT TO LIVE AND GROW. Without heat and light from the sun, plants would not survive. And without plant life, we would have no food to eat or oxygen to breathe.

Prove That Plants Need Light!

First Experiment

Step 1. Put a piece of wood on the grass.

Step 2. After a week take the wood away.

What do you notice? Is there any difference between the grass that was under the wood and the rest of the grass?

Why did the grass under the wood turn yellow or die?

What did the grass under the wood need in order to grow?

Second Experiment

Step 1. Fill two pots with soil. Plant seeds in the soil. (Try radish seeds—they grow quickly!)

Step 2. Put a can over one of the pots. Put both pots by the window.

Step 3. Water the seeds every day. After two weeks take the can off.

Did the seeds in both pots grow? Which pot of seeds grew?

Why did some seeds grow? Why did the other seeds not grow?

LIGHT MAKES SHADOWS. We can see through transparent items, such as glass, water, air, and some plastic. Each of these allows light to go through it. Light does not go through a wooden door, because wood is opaque. When a light shines on you, it does not go through you, because your body is opaque. When the light shines on you, there is a dark shape near you; that dark shape is your shadow.

Find and Make Shadows

Go outside on a sunny day. Look around you. A space near you is dark. That dark space is your shadow. It is shaped just like you, because your body blocks the light from going through it.

Try this:

Find the shadow of a house, a friend, a pet, or a tree.

Walk. Watch your shadow follow you. Jump. Watch your shadow jump.

Hold an action figure up to the light. Why is its shadow the same shape as the action figure?

Go outside early on a sunny morning. Have someone measure how long your shadow is. Write that number down. Go outside in the sunshine at noon. Have someone measure your shadow. Now compare the two numbers. Is the morning shadow longer than the noon shadow? Why is one shadow longer than the other?

This book meets the Common Core State Standards for Science and Technical Subjects.